ThrillCraft:

Story Structure for Unputdownable Crime Fiction

Tony McFadden

Copyright © 2023 Tony McFadden
All rights reserved.
ISBN: 978-0-6456733-1-9

If you're interested in more titles by this author, a list can be found at the end of this book.

DEDICATION

To all "aspiring" writers:

You're not "aspiring".

You're writers.

DISCLAIMER

This is *my* cut at story structure.

It's tailored specifically to crime fiction, mysteries, thrillers, and the like.

The concepts can apply to Romance, fantasy, comedy fiction and any other genre you can think of, but the terminology will not always be the same.

Also, I swear a bit in this book. Look away if that offends you.

Tony McFadden

ACKNOWLEDGMENTS

My introduction to story structure was at the hands of Larry Brookes.

Look for his stuff on StoryFix.com

It's good.

Structure

Introduction

For the past twelve years, I've been honing my writing skills, publishing (at the date of this publication) one non-fiction book — you're reading it — and eighteen novels.

I write mostly crime fiction. A couple of sci-fi books are in the mix, but the overall gist is crime.

- Private Investigators in Australia.
- Telecommunications Engineers in far-flung parts of the world sticking their noses where they shouldn't.
- A millionaire Irishman solving mob-related crimes in South Florida.
- A young Australian actress trying her damnedest to make a living in La-La-Land.

Structure

When I started, I knew nothing about CREATING a story. I'd read thousands by then. Some were great, some were awful, and most were just good.

I started writing my first book, **Matt's War**, with an interesting concept, believable characters, and no idea how it would end. I knew there should be a beginning, middle and end, but I had no idea what should happen in each of those three parts, what triggered the transition between them, and how much of the story each of those parts made up.

"Common sense" says the beginning is a third of the story, the middle is a third, and the end is a third.

Turns out, no.

I had a general idea of how the book should go. I definitely knew how it started. The rest, well, I trusted it would work itself out.

I finished the first draft after a couple of months. Okay, more like twelve months.

The story had an end. The characters had an arc. The good guys won, and the bad guys were punished (with a thin, hanging thread setting up a sequel).

But I ran into many familiar first-writer problems: A dead middle. Clues were revealed too early (or, in some cases, too late). It had an abrupt ending. It was on the bad side of the scale. Unfortunately (for me), it was a *story* I really liked.

I put it aside and started working on my second. **Family Matters**. (The second book I wrote, not the second book I released.)

It progressed in the same way. It had a good start, but I had NO idea how it would end; a middle so dead that I decided to have my main character shot to keep it interesting. And a really sloppy ending.

Around the same time I completed the first draft of Family Matters, I was introduced to the basics of story structure. I learned some important points about story telling. The key ones:

- The hero / main character needs to drive the conclusion. He or she can't be "rescued". (Not a structure thing, to be fair, but it drives the plot points.)
- Every critical character, weapon, characteristic, etc., should be introduced in Act One even if it's just a passing reference.
- NOTHING new (weapons, skills, people critical to the ending) should be introduced as late as Act 3.
- And a few other things that I'll get into throughout this little book.

All of this was new to me. But it resonated. This was a PLAN—a blueprint for the story, laying out the milestones along the journey. I'm an engineer by training, and an engineer likes nothing more than a plan.

I re-wrote Matt's War and Family Matters with the principles I outline in this book. Matt's War is still one of my favourites and sits at 4.5/5 stars on Amazon.

Family Matters is still a bit of a mess —too many plotlines make it a bit busy. But I still like it. And it is a massive improvement over the first draft. A reviewer on Amazon said, *"...I was hooked from the very first page. It was superbly written, fast paced and thrilling, straight to the point without frills."*

Everything (fiction) I write now is built around structure. I'll argue in this book how adhering to a structure doesn't mean cookie-cutter stories, and I'll also argue that once you are familiar and comfortable with the concept of structure, *you should forget it and write your story.*

But you have to understand its power first.

I've written eighteen books over the past dozen years. They all "follow" the structure laid out in this book. These guidelines keep your story pacy and on point. When writing a story, my goal is to have the reader start at point A, finish at a completely unrelated point Z, and wonder how in the hell they got there, yet at no point in that journey get pulled out of the story.

My readers seem to think I'm getting the hang of things:

"This is a fast read, interesting plot." – **Book 'Em** review.

"Very action packed, on the edge of your seat story." – **Broken** review

"It was so fast paced that sometimes I couldn't tell if the story advanced by one day, one week or one month. But it was really entertaining and definitely a page turner." – **Broken** review

"This is a short, fast read, …with lots of action, a few twists and turns, and several suspects to follow." – **Batteries Not Included** review.

"It's action-packed from start to finish with a twist or two to keep the reader engaged" – **Number Fifteen** review.

"As the case progresses, the plot gets more and more twisted, involving double cross, revenge, and manipulation. A fast read that's pretty much all on the surface like an action/adventure." – **The Murder of Jeremy Brookes** review.

And dozens more.

Making sure you hit the beats described in this book can ensure your story doesn't lag, and your readers don't toss your book on the DNF pile and reach for someone else's.

What this book *doesn't* do.

At no point will I talk about dangling participles, split infinitives or mismatched subject-verb pairs.

There are tons of how-to-write books. My best tip (if you're interested) is to read your brains out. Read your favourite genre. Read a genre you never would think of reading. Read as much as you can.

You'll see dozens of ways to express the passage of time, or how to effectively use dialogue tags.

My second best tip is to write. A lot. Find your voice. It's not Neil Gaiman's voice or Lee Child's voice. It's *your* voice.

And my third and final non-structure tip is to forestall edits until you've got your first draft in the bag. Don't interrupt the creative flow with niggling things like, what was it again? Split infinitive or incorrect verb tenses. That's for later.

This is not a long book. You should be writing, not reading about how to write. I could put together 400 pages of fluff, but I prefer meat and potatoes writing. This is quick and concise.

Full disclosure: I'm going to spoil a bunch of movies

and some books.

Movies:
- Tomorrow, When the War Began
- Limitless
- Witness
- Nobody
- A Knight's Tale
- Harry Potter and the Deathly Hallows (Part 1)

Books:
- Matt's War – Tony McFadden
- 61 Hours – Lee Child

Structure

Structure Overview

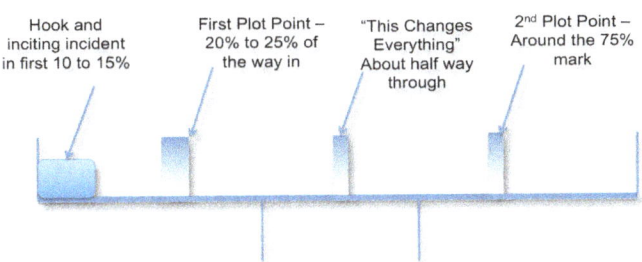

Pinch points. Let your inner bad-ass free

Much like all houses have floors, walls, windows and roofs, and much like all faces have a nose, mouth and two eyes, all stories have a structure. No two houses look the same (unless you're in one of those new, poorly built, looks-like-it's-designed-by-ChatGPT suburbs), no two faces look alike (I know, twins – analogies aren't perfect), and no two stories are the same. But they have the same backbone – the same framework.

The image at the top of this chapter sums up the basics of story structure:

- Act One to the First Plot Point,
- Act Two to the Second Plot Point,
- Act Three to the end and a resolution,
- "This Changes Everything" midpoint,
- and a couple of Pinch Points to keep the tension amped (more on those later).

This is a standard Three Act structure. The First Act ends about 20% to 25% into the story. The middle (roughly) half of the story is Act Two, and the final quarter (roughly) is Act Three.

When people see this, they initially think it makes all stories the same. How could a story possibly be original if you're following the same recipe?

Except it's not the recipe, so much as the instructions. Scaffolding to hang the story on. Originality is not determined by the architecture of the story. The structure is merely a set of guidelines for creating a story flow that readers will find comfortable. Originality comes from your compelling characters, interesting settings and unique events.

Act One is the setup. It establishes the main character in their *status quo*. It defines their particular world and establishes their place in it. It has to be substantial enough to ground the character in their reality firmly, but not so long that the reader gets bored. It ends with an event that throws the MC out of their status quo. The story actually starts here.

The first half of **Act Two** has our hero reacting to the new state they're in. From a character's point of view, they may be willing to proceed now, but they're unsure where to go. Until the **Midpoint**, where a critical new piece of information is revealed that more clearly defines their path.

Even though the hero makes progress through Act Two, they ultimately seem to fail. At one point, they *think* they're winning, but then it feels like nothing is working. Near the end of Act Two is the "**All is Lost**" moment. Dejected, beaten, bruised and battered, they are ready to throw in the towel until they get the final piece of the puzzle.

Then there's **Act Three**.

Act Three *starts* with the final piece of the puzzle. The end state is clear in your hero's eyes. The path to *get* to that end state still needs to be defined, but the destination is finally known. With all of the information now at hand, Act Three is essentially a series of obstacles to the final goal. Smaller obstacles are removed first, then larger and larger, until your hero faces the big boss.

The story ends when the story ends. Whatever it was that threw the hero out of their status quo is resolved. The hero drives the resolution. Ideally, the book's final scene should echo the opening scene to close the loop. There's more to the final chapter of the book than that, of course, but I cover that in the penultimate chapter of *this* book.

I cannot emphasise enough that there is no arbitrary preciseness with the length of each Act. If your book is 400 pages long, for example, Act One does not have to be exactly 100 pages long. Anywhere from 80 to 110 pages would do.

Shorter than that, though, and it's unlikely you'll have enough space to lay out the information critical to the success of your story. Longer than that, and you're delaying the story you need to tell. Get to it as quickly as possible, without leaving anything out.

The macro-benefit of story structure is the balance it brings to the final product.

In the coming chapters, I'll break each of these parts of the story down in more detail. I'm going to include examples, from books, or, more frequently, from movies. Movies are an easier medium to dissect.

This brings me to one final concern I've heard

about story structure: that it's only useful for the post-mortem of a story. That it's used to pull apart a completed work to show where the midpoint turn occurs, or what the first plot point is, but not to build one.

I heard that opinion from a highly respected screenwriter a few weeks ago. I still respect him, but I disagree.

It doesn't even make that much sense.

If you deconstruct a story to discover the structure, then the structure had to be part of the story's construction. Much in the same way that it's essential that all homes have doors and ceilings, and roofs. I guarantee you that every successful movie and book over the past century follows a structure like described herein, or one similar. If the author or screenwriter didn't do it intentionally, it was either a subconscious decision or a good editor who fixed it.

Trying to write crime fiction without knowing the path you will take is an exercise in excessive trial and error. The Midpoint twist needs to be related to the resolution, which means you need to know the resolution. The Inciting Incident needs to trigger the First Plot Point. Skills and clues, and characters essential to the story's resolution need to be introduced, even if only tangentially, in Act One.

It's a Chekov thing.

And, again, knowing story structure inside-out does not a good book make. It can make a good book great, but you still need to have a compelling story, a stable of interesting characters and an unexpected twist or two.

I'm a die-hard plotter, and I suggest taking the time to sort out what your story is before you start writing it. Even with the knowledge of good structure, if you don't plan first, you will spend a lot of time reviewing your manuscript, plugging plot holes and avoiding *Deus ex Machina* scenarios.

A little bit of planning goes a long way.

So let's go.

Act One

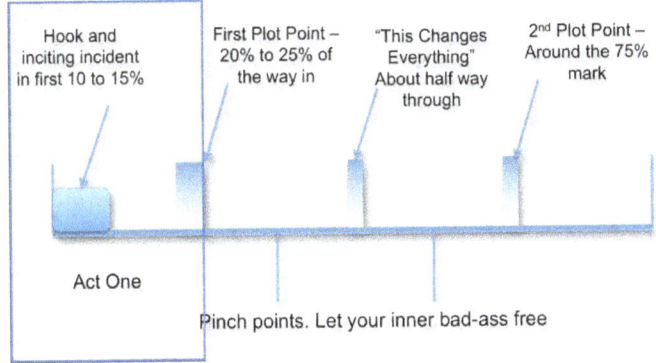

Before you take your reader on a journey with your hero, you need to set their baseline. An adventure is only an adventure if it's different from "normal".

So you need to establish "normal". That's what Act One is for. Even if you're writing book twelve in a series, you must assume the reader hasn't read books 1 through 11. Establish the normal. Introduce the main character's friends, if they contribute to the resolution. If weapons are used, at least mention their existence and the MC's skills with that weapon. Even if it's just in passing or a thinly-veiled hint.

I read a book by a very successful author a few years back that had the protagonist take out the main baddie by accurately throwing a baseball-sized rock at the baddie's head. He explained to his partner, afterwards, that he played college baseball and he had been a starting pitcher (or something along those lines). This happened in Act Three, and there was no mention of his college baseball experience or expertise before that point in the book. Big mistake. Took me completely out of the story.

Was it mentioned in previous books? I have no idea. I hadn't read them. Still haven't.

"Normal" doesn't mean *your* normal. It means normal for the main character. Unless, of course, the main character is an author trying to figure out their story.

Your main character's normal should be what they wake up to every morning. Do they have ongoing cases that need work? Are they in a contentious relationship with the police? Do they flirt with the grandmother in the bank? Is their hip fucked up from a stray round during a shoot-out five years ago? Have they just broken their wrist in a bicycling accident?

This is the opportunity to show your reader who your characters are. It's also a good place to seed some of your characters' capabilities and mannerisms that will be used later in the story to help drive the resolution.

Think of the opening scenes in the movie **Tomorrow, When the War Began**. Normal is regional Australia, seven friends planning a camping trip away. In **Limitless**, Eddie Morra is struggling to get a single word written the book he's contracted to write, life slowly turning to shambles. In **Witness**, normal is Book's day-to-day cop life in Philly, responding to a murder in a train station bathroom.

The first act is also the place to introduce any internal conflicts the protagonist may have. Through the story's arc, they will be forced to face those internal conflicts and come to grips with them.

Along with introducing your hero and all of their friends and allies, Act One is also where the *antagonists'* normal is defined.

What nefarious deeds make up *their* day-to-day? What are they planning, blind to the forces of good that will be marshalled against them making (don't give too much away, yet)?

While not structure-related, it's always good to make your villains' drive to do what they do as compelling as the hero's. Add depth to the villains. Their home life. Why they do what they do. Why they don't do what they don't do? Any alliances they might have that could come in handy later in the story.

Build their whole world.

There's a lot to cover in the first act. Even the weather if it plays a part in the story's resolution. If your story spans a few days and there's a huge storm informing events at the conclusion, the storm's forecast needs to come up in conversation.

In one of my books, a main character sees incriminating evidence while leaving jury duty. This happened late in Act Two and drove the resolution. Her jury duty was mentioned as a complaint about having to attend on the first page of Act One, then never mentioned until the jury duty scenes.

The end of Act One has your hero going through that metaphorical door into the "story". Don't have that be a surprise for the reader. The MC, and the reader, need to see that door coming for miles. They need to be "invited" through that door and initially reject it, preferring the comfort of their status quo.

Their reasons for rejecting the journey can be valid, or selfish, or whatever you, the author, need them to be to help develop character, but they need to initially reject it.

In **Nobody**, Hutch resists going through the door to his violent past because of his family, something he values above all. After a home invasion he essentially leaves well enough alone. Nothing valuable, as far as he knows, was taken.

In **A Knight's Tale**, William Thatcher takes over for his dead knight with the intent of making enough money to get back home, and then quitting.

Later in the first Act, something more compelling will entice or force them through that door. As the author, it's up to you to determine what it is. It could be a flight of fancy. It could be the urge to save a child. It's absolutely got to be related to the overall story, and it's got to be a one-way journey.

Your hero goes through that door, and they can't go back. For any reason. (Or you wouldn't have a story, right?)

Nobody has Hutch's daughter looking for her "kitty cat bracelet" and Hutch realises that the two punks who invaded his home took it.

And he has to track them down and get it back

Thatcher, in **A Knight's Tale** sees the woman who

he believes will be the love of his life. He's not going to stop "knighting" now. He's doing it for her. For love. He has a new reason to be a knight.

Act One is finished. And then the *real* story begins.

The next two chapters will discuss the Hook and the Inciting Incident, why they need to exist, and where they should sit in Act One.

The Hook

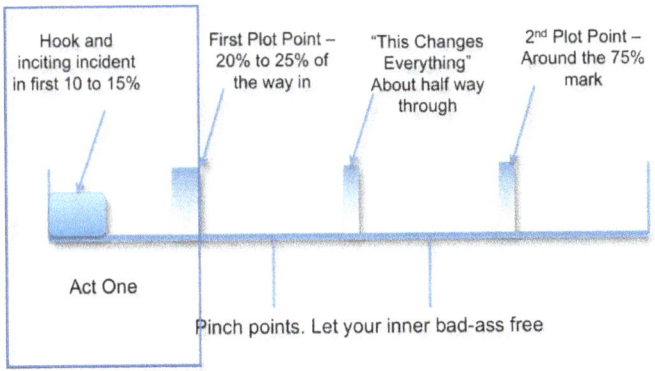

How often have you started a book and DNFd it because it didn't "get going"? Or started watching something on Netflix and skip to the next show in the queue because it had a slow start?

There is competition for eyeballs. You must grab your audience early, or they will bounce to the next best thing.

You need to **Hook** them. You need to make your reader settle in and accept the journey they are about to embark on from page one. From the first sentence, if you're good. And that opening hook doesn't *need* to relate even remotely to the main story.

Although it *can* be. More on that a bit later.

The **James Bond** franchise has this aced. The dapper spy opens every movie with an action sequence – sometimes related to the larger story, sometimes stand-alone – that nails you to the screen. And honestly, it doesn't matter whether the hook is related to the movie or not. It's thrilling. You settle into your seat and start eating popcorn.

In **Tomorrow Never Dies**, James Bond is at an arms bazaar on the Russian border. It's packed with all the world's best terrorists. He's confirmed that they are there, with weapons of all sorts, and HQ sends in a cruise missile to take them all out. He's got four minutes to clear out or be toast.

Then they see there are nukes strapped to the wings of a fighter jet. And they can't stop the missile.

Defying many laws of both physics and probability, Bond fights off the terrorists and steals the jet with the nukes just in the nick of time.

All in the first ten minutes. You're hooked.

But you're a writer. You need to do that with words.

The perfect writer does that with a perfect first line. I have yet to create such a thing. Maybe one day I will. If you can create such a thing, stop reading this now and go, write your book. You don't need me. Go. Write.

You're still here?

Okay.

Some of my favourite first sentences:

In Annie Hauxwell's *A Bitter Taste*: **"She was ten years old, but knew enough to wipe clean the handle of the bloody kitchen knife."**

Or Warren Ellis's *Crooked Little Vein*: **"I opened my eyes to see the rat taking a piss in my coffee mug."**

Or from my *A Step Too Far*: **"Jesus, but it was hot. Like two rats fucking in a wool sock, hot."**

I'll give you a tip: I re-write my first chapter after completing the first draft. I know the characters better, the story's conclusion, and what key points need to be emphasised. It's good form to have your last scene mirror your first scene. When you're writing your first scene, you still don't know what the last scene is. Once you're finished the first draft, though, you should have a better idea. Really, you should. They'll change through the editing process, but you'll still be able to link them.

It's been said: "Enter a scene as late as possible and leave as soon as possible." Excellent advice. Especially true for the first sentence of the first scene of the first chapter.

There's also a concept some people call "Save the cat". It's a scene showing your hero performing a selfless act early in the book to show the reader they are someone to be trusted. (See the opening scene in **Nobody**.)

It's a bit cliche. I prefer a very early scene that shows the reader exactly who the main character is. Action, if possible. Funny is even better. Profane, comedic action is the best. At least for the type of books I write.

One form of hook that is used, *mostly* ineffectively, is to show the all-is-lost moment at the end of Act Two (skip ahead if you want to read what that is), leave it as a cliff-hanger, then "Three Days Earlier" back to the beginning of the story, setting up tension in the reader, wondering a) how the main character gets to that moment and b) how they satisfactorily resolve the problem.

Sometimes it works; sometimes, it doesn't.

A good example of this technique that works (at

least I think it does) is from the movie "**Limitless**".

The movie starts with the story's hero Eddie Morra standing on a ledge on his balcony overlooking traffic many stories below. Russian mobsters are trying to get into his apartment. Trying very hard to get into his apartment. They're not there for a surprise birthday party.

Will he jump? Does he find a way out of the situation? The scene ends with him on the ledge, Russians in the apartment, and his life seemingly over.

The viewer has to watch almost 80 minutes of the movie to get to that opening scene and see how Eddie Mora solves his really very, extremely immediate problem.

It works, mostly because Bradley Cooper plays an engaging Morra. I'm not sure if it would work with anyone else in that role.

In **Nobody**, we go even farther into the story, opening the movie with what ends up being almost the final scene of the movie. Hutch is in interrogation, beat up, lighting a cigarette and **then opening a small can of tuna for a kitten he pulls from inside his jacket**.

"Who the fuck are you?" asks one of the interrogators.
"Me? I'm nobody."

In **Tomorrow, When the War Began**, we start with a recording made by Ellie, the main character, telling us a story about *"some of the things we've done, the friends we lost...there's only one way to do this: to go back to where it all began."*

On the second page of my first book, **Matt's War**, my main character, Matt Daly, and his sidekick George, interrupt a hijacking out of Singapore's Changi Airport.

Find your voice and let the reader know what it is from the jump. Make them want to read more.

Inciting Incident

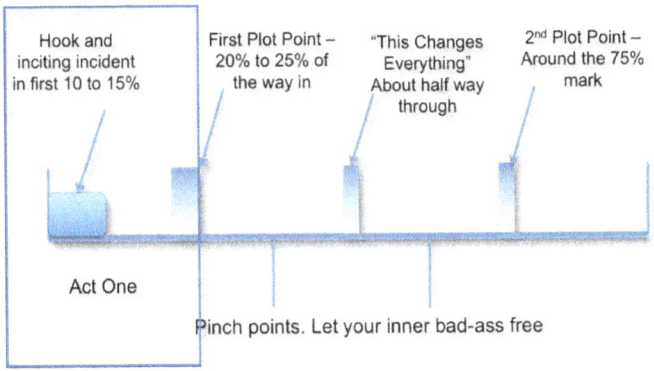

You know by now that the end of Act One has the protagonist leaving their status quo, through a metaphorical door into their new state. A big mistake many new writers make is not creating a path to that door early enough in the story to make that transition believable. There's nothing worse than requiring a reader to suspend all disbelief this early in your story. Show them the start of that path early in your book.

The start of this path is called the "Inciting Incident". If the villain shooting a cannon is the first plot point, the inciting incident is somebody lighting the fuse.

Maybe that's a bit too metaphorical.

If the First Plot Point is the rocket taking our hero into space, the Inciting Incident is the suggestion (which she initially turns down) that, due to her excellent scores in her aptitude test, she is perfectly suited to become an astronaut.

Ideally, your inciting incident should be subtle. It's better for the reader to see the first plot point and go: "Oh! *That's* why that happened."

The inciting incident in **Nobody** is the home invasion that Hutch essentially lets happen, to his son's disgust and his neighbour's ridicule.

In **Witness,** it's Samuel, hidden in a toilet stall, witnessing the cop's murder.

In **Tomorrow, When the War Began,** the teenagers are camping when they are woken one night by a sky full of aeroplanes heading toward their homes.

In my book **Matt's War**, the inciting incident is the

organisers of the failed hijacking realising who interrupted the hijacking, and that he is on an incoming flight to Malaysia. Where they will meet him.

The hero doesn't *need* to know what the inciting incident is, but the reader does.

First Plot Point

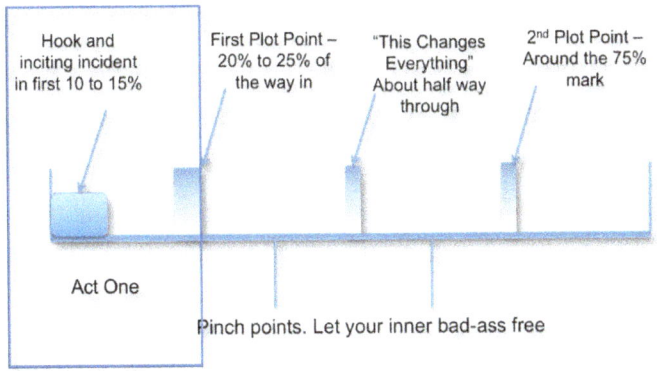

I've mentioned the First Plot Point a couple of times now. It's a major part of your story. It's a single thought, action, or nudge that moves your main character from their status quo to their new state.

Sometimes your hero actively resists the transition to hero. But they have no choice.

Something needs to be done, and they're the only person who can.

Or will.

The realisation that they are the chosen one (to overuse an already overused trope) is the First Plot Point.

Sometimes the hero is busting to start the adventure, but something is holding them back. It could be responsibilities, financial constraints or something else. That's the first plot point -- when they break through that thing holding them back.

In **Tomorrow, When the War Began**, there's a hint midway through Act One, the morning after the flyover, when one of the characters says, *"Maybe they weren't even ours."*

Hutch, in **Nobody**, actively resists returning to his "auditor" days until the point where he finds out his daughter's bracelet was one of the items stolen.

Remember, it can't come out of nowhere. It needs to be an option early in Act One. An option that is initially either rejected or refused or, at the time, seemingly impossible. The reader needs to know it's coming, anticipating the story, but not sure how it's going to happen. Build up the tension.

The second half of Act One builds tension, a "will she or won't she" tension that will clearly resolve to "she will", (or there wouldn't be any point for a reader to continue with your story).

But keep the reader guessing. Give your hero convincing excuses not to proceed until the hammer hits them (again, usually metaphorically) between the eyes

Then the First Plot Point releases that tension and starts the compression on a whole new spring.

It works best when the first plot point is character-based, and not prop based. For example, the First Plot Point in **Limitless** isn't Eddie getting the first pill, it's the realisation that the key to his future success is tied up in continued use of the pill, and then *keeping the existence of the pills he found from the police.*

The teenagers in **Tomorrow, When the War Began**, enter their new normal when they arrive home from a camping trip and find their homes deserted. Ellie (our hero) finds her dog dead. They sneak through the town and discover everyone is being held at the local showground by a foreign military force.

Witness has Samuel, the young Amish boy/witness discover a newspaper clipping in the squad room featuring the man he saw at the killing. Book realises a fellow cop (McFee) is involved.

In my book, **Matt's War,** the First Plot Point, the end of Act One, happens with Matt is abducted outside his Malaysian office the night he landed.

Act Two - First Half

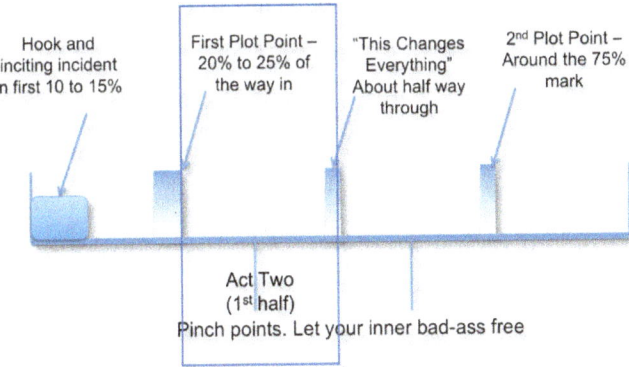

Okay, now the real story begins. Your hero is in the mix of it. The door is behind them, and the journey they either were dying to begin or fought to avoid has begun.

They won't know what's going on at first. Remember, this is no longer their status quo. They are in a world or situation they are not entirely familiar with. They, and the reader, will have a lot of questions. Questions, if unanswered, will make it difficult for the reader to suspend their disbelief.

Get those readers' obvious questions out of the way quickly.

Why doesn't the hero go to the police? Have a believable reason why not.

Maybe the police have already been involved and declared the death a suicide. The hero knows (but can't yet prove) that it was murder.

Or use an unreliable character. Your private detective's client could be lying to them.

As you go through this part of your story, think of all of the "yeah, but…" questions that would come to any reasonable reader's mind, and answer them.

Basically, what are the obvious solutions to the problem facing your hero (or, by extension, their client if they are a PI)? Discount those solutions early in Act Two.

After all, if the police can easily handle the problem, you don't have a story. The hero needs a valid reason to continue, so, as the creator of this tale, create plausible reasons to force your hero on their journey.

Your hero must go through each problem, one at a time, and fail at solving them. Or, at least, fail at solving the critical ones. Through those failures, they will learn more. More about themselves, more about the antagonist, more about the situation they now find themselves in.

With the knowledge gained from failure, they create a more grandiose plan. As they put this plan into action, sometimes it fails, making things worse. Along the way, they collect more information. Some of it is real, and some of it isn't. Maybe an unreliable witness tells them things that are wrong, either intentionally or as a well-meaning mistake.

In **Tomorrow, When the War Began**, the teenagers are trying to stay undetected while they figure out what to do. They move around under the cover of darkness, looking for weaknesses, very aware of their vulnerability.

Morra, in **Limitless**, is on top of the world. The pills are pushing him to unimagined heights. He's making money hand over fist and loving life. Everything is perfect, right?

Matt, in **Matt's War**, is not having it so well. He's locked in a hut in the Malaysian jungle somewhere, with another captive, a British businessman named Peter Stevenson. Initial activities involve trying, unsuccessfully, to escape.

Before we get to the end of the first half of Act Two

(that's a mouthful, right?), there's a useful narrative point, called a Pinch Point, that lets your readers (and sometimes your hero) know exactly what your hero is up against

That's the next chapter.

.

First Pinch Point

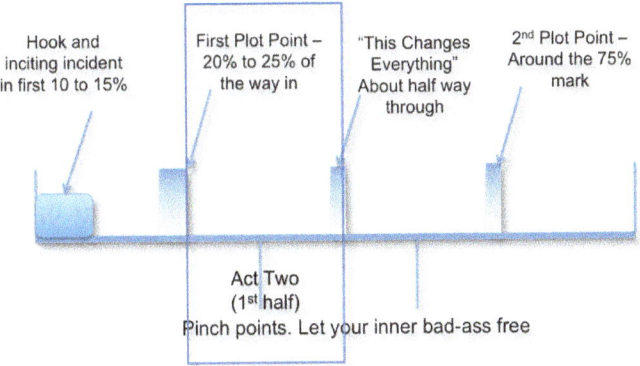

As your hero muddles their way through the first half of Act Two, slowly getting closer to the answer, it's useful to have an event that articulates for the reader, and sometimes the hero, what or who they are actually up against.

In the context of storytelling, a pinch point can

serve to remind the hero of the central conflict, reinforce for them why they embarked on the journey, increase the stakes, and add tension to the narrative. As a writer, it's an opportunity to let your inner badass free.

While the specifics can vary depending on the story and its structure, the first pinch point in a thriller typically involves some critical elements.

The first pinch point highlights the presence and power of the antagonistic force, which could be a villain, an opposing group, or an imminent threat. It showcases their actions, motivations, or impact on the protagonist's world, re-establishing the danger they pose.

In the **Tomorrow When the War Began**, the first pinch point is when the kids see the leader of the enemy forces shoot one of the townspeople at the showground in the head. Almost immediately after, two foreign fighter jets shoot down an Australian jet. It clarifies for them exactly what their opponent will do to win.

The pinch point in **Limitless** is a bit more subtle. Morra experiences his first side effect of the pill – a time skip. NZT (the drug in the pill) may *not* be the perfect solution to his problems.

The pinch point in **Nobody** is for the viewer only.

We see how violent Yulian, the Russian mob boss is. Hutch isn't aware of this, making the tension that little bit thicker.

Use the First Pinch Point to intensify the conflict in your story. Have your hero encounter obstacles and setbacks, or confront the baddie directly. This escalation creates a sense of urgency and raises the stakes, increasing the tension for both the hero and your readers.

You can also use the first pinch point as an opportunity to drop a couple of clues. Maybe a fake one to lead the reader astray. Or perhaps your hero gets their eyes on who they think is the main villain. New information about the antagonist's capabilities, a secret plot, or a revelation about a character's true nature. This revelation amplifies the danger and adds a new layer of complexity to the story.

On the other side of the pinch point, the hero, sometimes, will have some new information. The reader definitely will. How they use it is up to you, the author. More pieces of the puzzle. It's handy if a subtle clue or two found here can be called back at the resolution.

Remember, the specifics of the first pinch point can vary depending on the story and your creative choices. The aim is to inject a sense of urgency, and increase the tension as the story progresses.

The best pinch point I have read in a book was in **61 Hours**, by Lee Child. The hero (Jack Reacher) isn't aware of this pinch point, but the reader is, and it's the reader that needs to know what the stakes are.

In the book, it's mentioned that the bad guy is short, with a vicious temper. To illustrate the viciousness of his temper, he cuts the lower part of a minion's legs off, after that minion mocked him for his short stature. He cut off enough leg to ensure the minion was now shorter than the boss.

Reacher doesn't get this message. The reader does, setting the stakes for the battle that will inevitably come.

In **Matt's War**, Matt isn't aware of the first pinch point. He's unconscious in the shack. His co-prisoner, Peter, harasses one of the terrorists, trying to get medical help for Matt, and is kicked in the ribs for his troubles. The bad guys want them alive, not necessarily healthy.

MidPoint Turn

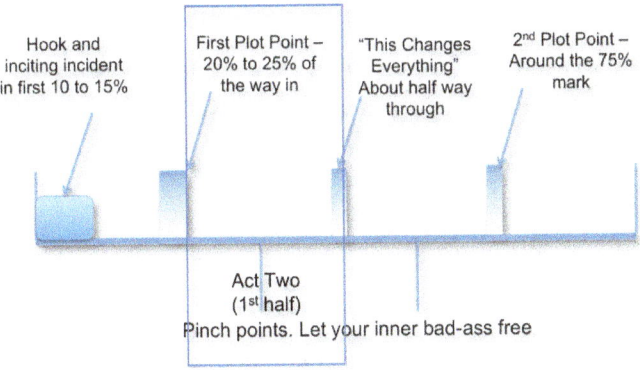

The Midpoint Turn, the "this changes everything" moment, is a pivotal point in the story marking a significant shift in the narrative, often changing the plot's direction and altering the hero's understanding of the conflict. Your hero is blazing, full steam ahead, down a path they believe leads to the resolution and something or someone knocks them off that path onto another. It's a "What the -?" moment for the protagonist and the reader.

It literally is a major piece of information unearthed by the hero that makes them realise they've been heading down the wrong path.

A special example is the two-part movie that makes up **Harry Potter and the Deathly Hallows**. The book's Midpoint Turn, the "this changes everything" moment for Harry Potter, happens at the *end* of the 7th movie.

The end of the first movie is the midpoint of the total story. The movie ends with Voldemort cracking open Dumbledore's coffin and snagging his wand. That action changes the story going forward (as we see in the second movie).

In Lee Child's book **61 Hours**, the midpoint occurs when Reacher learns that the military bunker that is the focus of the book isn't an Army Base like he thought, but an Air Force Base.

In fact, Childs has Reacher actually say "This changes everything."

Because it does. And this is a nice subtle midpoint because the *hero* knows why it changes everything, but the reader needs a little more reading time to understand why.

This twist can't just be tossed in by the author unless there's been a good bit of planning first. In fact, a good story will have some ambiguous clues interpreted by the hero (or other characters) so that the twist has more impact. Everything up to this point has the hero striving for outcome "A". This twist requires him to abandon "A" and start striving for "B".

Take your favourite book (this is most obvious in thriller or suspense novels) and crack it open to the book's midpoint. I can almost 100% guarantee you that you'll find a scene a few pages either side of the middle (e.g., somewhere between pages 180 to 220 of a 400 page book) that "changes everything".

The midpoint turn typically raises the stakes and escalates the conflict. It may involve a sudden increase in danger, a setback for the protagonist, or a revelation that reveals the true extent of the threat they face. This escalation creates tension and propels the story into higher-stakes territory.

Morra finds out, at **Limitless**'s midpoint, that withdrawal from the drug is fatal, and he just ran out.

Ellie and one of her teenage friends realise that the key to the success of invasion in **Tomorrow, When the War Began,** was a bridge from the port to the rest of Australia. They're unsure what to do about it yet, but it's a vital, new piece of information.

In **Matt's War**, the new information Matt and his shack-mate Peter receive is that their ultimate destination is as involuntary suicide bombers against their respective (American and British) Embassies.

Act Two - Second Half

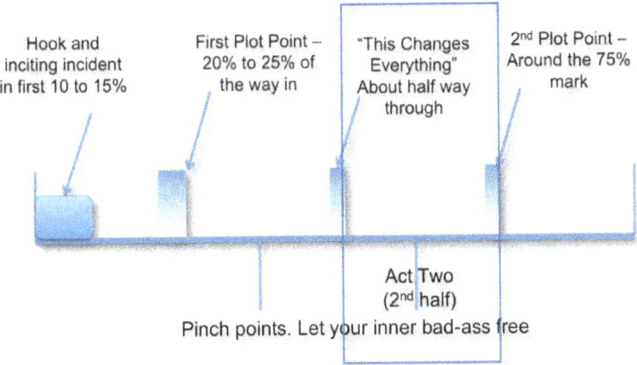

We're in the second half of the book, now. Your hero has a lot more information. They realise they've made mistakes. Some of those mistakes may have cost them. Your hero doesn't need to come out of the end of this journey unscathed. Knock them around a bit.

There's less hesitation and more deliberation in this part of the story. A significant amount of information (but not all of it) is in your hero's hands. Leave a few key pieces out, though. You'll need them at the end of Act Two.

The conflict intensifies with the information they have, and the hero faces more significant challenges, obstacles, or direct confrontations with the villain's henchmen. The tension mounts as they struggle to overcome these hurdles.

Important secrets or betrayals may be revealed during this part of the story. These revelations add complexity, deepen the intrigue, and shake the protagonist's understanding of the situation. They may involve unexpected alliances, unexpected motivations, or the unmasking of hidden agendas.

The last half of Act Two is a good place for further character development, allowing the audience to gain deeper insights into the hero and the villain. Their strengths, vulnerabilities, and internal conflicts may be explored, making them more multidimensional and relatable.

The hero's options are getting difficult by this point in the story. The obvious solutions have been examined and discarded. The capabilities of the villain are more apparent than ever. We have a second pinch point in the middle of this section (more in the next chapter) that amplifies the danger and raises the stakes even further. The hero may face moral dilemmas, lose key resources or allies, or encounter unexpected setbacks. These challenges force them to adapt, think creatively, or take risks to move forward.

The story may include surprising twists or reversals that subvert the audience's expectations. A henchman decides to flip, or the main villain's identity is finally revealed with surprising results. These twists keep the audience engaged and heighten the suspense as the story unfolds unexpectedly.

We're setting everything up here for the climax of the story. The puzzle pieces start coming together, and the protagonist's final plan or confrontation with the antagonist takes shape. The tension continues to rise as the story hurtles towards the climax.

Morra is on a rollercoaster at this point in **Limitless**. His pills have been stolen, more people are against him than he realised, and he's tanked the merger of a lifetime – one that would make him $40 million. But he knows who is against him now. It's not just the Russians. The shadowy figure on the other side of the merger has sent muscle after him to get the pills.

Ellie and her friends are escalating their attempts to free friends and take out the enemy in **Tomorrow, When the War Began**, with Ellie's driving skills used to steal a garbage truck to rescue injured friends.

In **Matt's War**, Matt and his co-captor ramp up their attempts to escape, and friendly external forces are getting closer.

Second Pinch Point

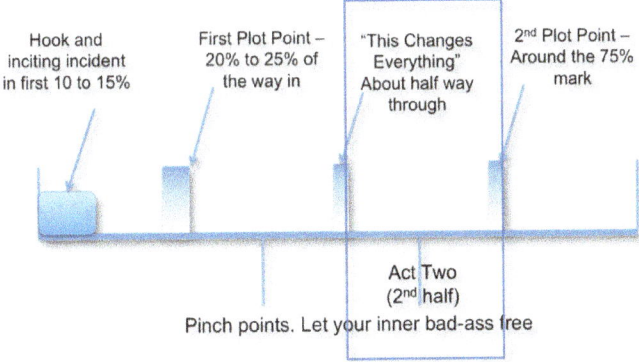

Pinch points. Let your inner bad-ass free

We had a pinch point in the first half of Act Two, and we have a pinch point in the second half of Act Two.

We still use this scene to amplify how determined/evil/nefarious the villain is, similar to the First Pinch Point. But we add a bit of spice to this one.

By now, the hero knows the depths the villain will plumb to succeed. But the hero isn't willing to quit. The scene is a battle the hero doesn't back away from. He can't win, yet, but he can get a good kick or two in.

The Second Pinch Point reminds the protagonist and the readers of the power, threat, or presence of the antagonistic force. It showcases the villain's capabilities, cunning, or impact on the protagonist's world, underscoring the danger the protagonist faces.

The Second Pinch Point introduces new complications, obstacles, or setbacks for the hero. It may involve unexpected betrayals, unforeseen challenges, or revelations that disadvantage the protagonist. Complications that test the hero's resilience and resourcefulness.

You should take the opportunity at this pinch point to give your hero some existential grief. It may involve a moment of doubt, a crisis of faith, or a difficult decision that pushes the protagonist to their limits. This emotional journey deepens the character's development and adds further complexity to the story.

The Second Pinch Point also sets the stage for the final confrontation between the protagonist and the antagonist. It creates a sense of urgency, propelling the story towards the climax.

I like using the Second Pinch Point in my books to demonstrate how far the hero(s) will go to succeed.

In **Tomorrow, When the War Began**, Ellie is driving a garbage truck when bad guys in buggies start chasing her and shooting at her. With her driving skills, she manages to evade and destroy them spectacularly, demonstrating her enhanced willingness to take the battle to them.

In **Witness**, the second pinch point occurs when the crooked captain grills Book's partner, Carter. The captain knows Carter has been in contact with Book, and Carter knows the captain is crooked. Again, it's subtle. We see it. Book doesn't.

Morra's girlfriend in **Limitless** has gone to get his pill stash for him, and on the way back is followed by the muscle trying to steal it. Morra gets her to take one of the pills and she fights her way to freedom. Not subtle.

Structure

All is Lost

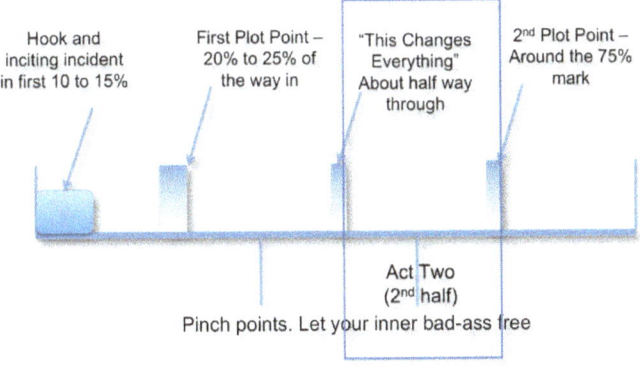

We're not out of Act Two yet. The "All Is Lost" moment, also known as the "Dark Night of the Soul" or the "Lowest Point," is a critical moment in the narrative of any good story. It occurs towards the end of Act Two, and is characterised by a significant setback or loss for the your hero. The hero and his team are convinced they have lost. The villain is convinced they have won. This setback can take various forms, such as the apparent death of a loved one, the hero's capture, the revelation of a devastating truth, or the collapse of the hero's plan.

The "All Is Lost" moment plunges the hero into deep despair, hopelessness, or confusion. They question their abilities, lose faith in their mission, and struggle with self-doubt. This emotional turmoil further intensifies the impact of the setback.

The hero may also lose crucial resources, allies, or support during this moment. They might lose key information, lose the trust of important allies, or find themselves isolated and without the means to achieve their goal.

The "All Is Lost" moment often presents your hero with a seemingly impossible situation and limited options for recovery. All avenues for success have been exhausted, leaving the hero with little hope of overcoming their obstacles.

This moment serves as a turning point for the protagonist. It forces them to confront their deepest fears, and flaws, or re-evaluate their motivations. It pushes them to their lowest point and challenges them to find the strength to rise above their circumstances.

The "All Is Lost" moment acts as a bridge between the second act and the climax of the story. It sets up the final act by creating a heightened sense of urgency and the need for a dramatic resolution.

We already know Morra's all-is-lost moment in **Limitless**. He's on his balcony, waiting for the Russians, and weighing the option of jumping over fighting. It's how the movie opens.

Book's all-is-lost moment in **Witness** occurs when he calls his partner from Amish land and finds out he's "been killed in the line of duty". His only secure link to the police has been cut. He's on his own, with little or no idea how or when the attack is coming.

The "All Is Lost" moment aims to increase the stakes, deepen the conflict, and test the protagonist's resolve. It often sets the stage for a powerful comeback, where the protagonist gathers their strength and embarks on the final push towards the resolution of the thriller.

Your hero should be bloodied, bruised, near death and on the run. The previous chapters should lead up (or, more accurately, down) to that "all is lost" point. Then, after allowing the briefest of hero wallowing, along comes the Second Plot Point.

The final clue, the last piece of the puzzle, the

incentive to go those final yards, that's the Second Plot Point.

Maybe your hero knows the bad guy killed her best friend and set it up to look like a suicide. Absolutely, positively knows. But can't prove it.

The Second Plot Point provides the proof. Maybe it's something in the background of a picture, or some other piece of evidence hidden until this point.

Matt's all-is-lost in **Matt's War** occurs at the end of Act Two when he thrown in the back of a panel van with Peter, taken to be strapped into a remote-control, explosive-laden van and pointed to their respective embassies.

In **Nobody**, Hutch is a lone warrior against an overwhelming force and seemingly impossible odds.

Plan the preceding chapters so a natural discovery reveals all and sets in motion the book's final chapters.

Second Plot Point

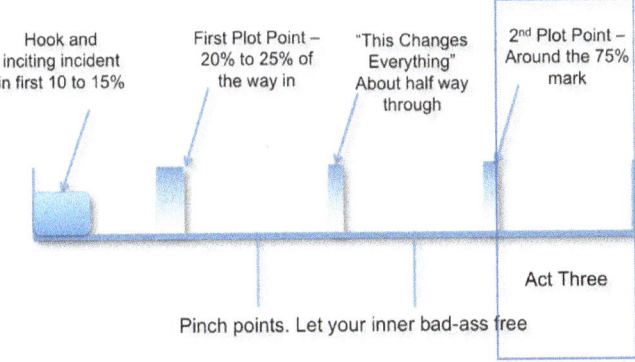

If the First Plot Point at the end of Act One was what compelled your hero to breach the metaphorical door to the "story", the Second Plot Point, at the end of Act Two, is the final piece of the puzzle, leading them to the resolution.

They are in their all-is-lost place, and something needs to pull them out of it and drive them on to their finale and, if you want a sequel, keep them alive.

How this final piece of information is presented is up to you. It doesn't even need to be a piece of information. It can be a reminder of what's at stake. A sight they hadn't seen in a long time, or an email from an old friend.

Maybe your hero knows the bad guy killed her best friend and set it up to look like a suicide. Absolutely, positively knows. But can't prove it.

The Second Plot Point provides the proof. Maybe it's something in the background of a picture, or a recording left by the victim just discovered by your hero.

Plan the preceding chapters so a natural discovery reveals all and sets in motion the final quarter of the book.

It's a subtle thing in **Tomorrow, When the War Began**. The team realise the best thing they can do for the war effort is to take out the bridge. All of their activities after this drive to that result.

Morra remembers that he has one pill left in **Limitless**. That's enough to get him off the ledge we saw him on at the opening, and on to a fight for survival.

In **Matt's War**, the terrorist has Matt and Pete in

the back of a van. He thinks they're unconscious, but Matt didn't get a full dose (an error made by the terrorist earlier in Act Two). Matt has enough presence of mind to start planning an escape.

In all cases, the Second Plot Point doesn't resolve the story. It tells the hero what is required to resolve the story. There's still a hard yard of work for them to do.

In Act Three.

Structure

Act Three

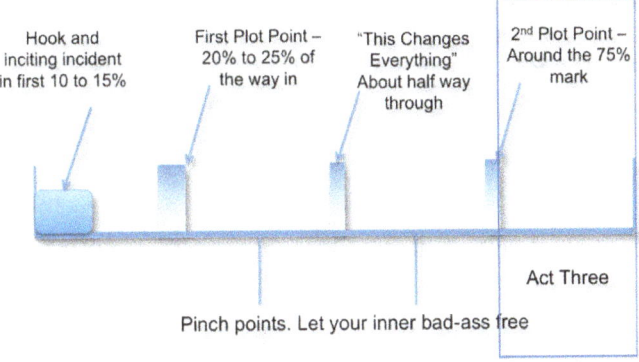

You have reached Act Three.

According to textbooks, in Act Three, the story reaches its climax and moves towards its resolution. This is the final act of the narrative.

And that tells you **next to nothing** as far as your story goes. So let's set up where we are…

- Your characters should all now be well-defined. Your readers have "discovered" their strengths and weaknesses, what makes them tick and their hidden fears and desires,
- Your hero believes they know what they're up against – they believe they have the problem sorted out, they need to push through to the end,
- Your villain (and their henchmen) should be rattled, but convinced of success. The hero has given them a run for their money, but they've held him off so far, and there are plans to take him out once and for good,
- It's crucial that from this point forward, no new information, people or clues that directly drive the conclusion are introduced. Everything the hero needs should be already present. This doesn't mean the clues have to be obvious. A picture seen in Act One could be the thing that tips events in our hero's favour.

Not all of the work is complete yet, though. Not for you, the author, not for the hero, and not for the readers.

The biggest hill is still in front of the hero, waiting

to be climbed. She marshals her forces, and attacks who or what she thinks is the ultimate villain.

There's a battle. Biggest battle of the book so far. (So. Far.) Lives might be lost on both sides. Hearts could be broken. Whatever happens, the hero will come out of the other side with a false sense of accomplishment. Because on the other side, she will discover the final, all-or-nothing, hurdle.

THAT battle will be a doozy. In some cases, it's life or death.

Now it's not unheard of to have your hero die saving the world (or whatever sliver of the world is important to them). Makes sequels difficult, but it's a valid ending. As long as that death serves the story.

Seems, as written, that Act Three can be a single chapter long. Maximum two. Not a lot to do, right?

Oh, it's never that easy.

Frankly, when I'm plotting/planning my books I leave the bulk of Act Three's planning until I've written the first draft of Acts One and Two. The basic Act Three things I know at the outset are who the baddie is, where I *expect* the final battle to play out, any allies who may have fallen along the way (temporarily or permanently) and the actual mechanism used to defeat the antagonist.

I'm unsure of anything more than that before I get to the end of Act Two.

And much of that "planned" Act Three will not last. It serves as a guidepost while writing my first draft, but more information is known by the end of Act Two.

And that information is important to how Act Three develops. You're hero, as already stated, has the information they need to complete the job. In the penultimate battle, they'll realise the little things earlier in the story will ultimately help them in what will be the final battle. A weak spot or a blind spot and some other small advantage they can use.

It's up to you, but I suggest putting Act Three planning to one side until you've finished the first draft of Acts One and Two.

The bridge is the objective in **Tomorrow, When the War Began**. Ellie steals petrol tanker truck, while her friends cause a large herd of cattle to stampede over the bridge, distracting the sentries. She parks the petrol truck under one end of the bridge and blows it up, taking out the bridge.

But it's a long road to get there. There's a huge battle to get the truck, and a bigger battle to get the truck lit up. Friends are injured, sacrifices are made, and not everyone escapes.

And we end back at the recording from the beginning. It's war. They're a guerrilla operation

Eddie Morra gets enough **Limitless** drug into him to sort out the Russians and get his hands on his stash, and we flash to Twelve Months Later, where he's running for Senate, and, using the knowledge gained from being on the Limitless drug, has tweaked the formula so he could wean himself off without any negative consequences.

Matt's War concludes with Matt extricating himself from his van, warning the right people about Peter's truck bomb, and using his telecommunications expertise to defuse *his* truck bomb. It takes roughly 20,000 words to get to that point.

This can't be done in a couple of chapters. Once the key piece of info is revealed at the end of Act Two, your hero needs to set up their plans. They'll have to get through ever-increasing obstacles until they reach their penultimate battle. Then, basking in success, discover one more hurdle to overcome.

And you need to make your reader believe that no coincidence, *deus ex mac*hina or luck was involved. It has to be honest.

And if you can wrap it up with a closing scene that ties up all the threads while mirroring the opening scene, so much the better.

The ending of **Tomorrow, When the War Began** is back to Ellie's recording

The ending of **Limitless** has Morra in control of his life, the knowledge gained from the pill put to good use.

Final Chapter

As a writer, getting to this chapter is immense relief. You've written the end of your book. There's a temptation to rush this chapter, for no other reason than the desperate urge to get to those magic two words – "The End".

Resist the urge. This is the chapter that your reader will remember. This is the chapter that your reader will use to decide whether they will go for your next book. Make it count.

This is the clean-up chapter. The main battle has occurred. I'm assuming, for the sake of argument, you've let your hero live another day, ready for the sequel after a bit of rest.

Allow emotional closure for your characters. Show their reactions to the outcome of the conflict, their personal growth, or their reconciliation with the events that unfolded. Emotions such as relief, satisfaction, or grief may be explored as characters come to terms with their experiences.

Include a final revelation or twist that provides a last-minute surprise for the reader. These can be additional layers of the mystery, unexpected character motivations, or the unveiling of hidden truths. These revelations add depth and intrigue to the final chapter.

You might include an epilogue or an aftermath section that glimpses into the characters' lives after the main conflict. It could show how they've moved forward, the consequences of their actions, or the impact of the events on their future. This section can offer a sense of closure and show the aftermath of the thrilling journey.

The final chapter of your book brings the narrative to a satisfying conclusion, wrapping up the storylines and leaving the reader with a sense of resolution. It's the last opportunity to leave a lasting impact and hook them into buying your next book (after leaving an awesome review).

So what, from here?

So now what?

After my second book, I learned that it helps the writing process immeasurably if I spend enough time plotting out my stories before I write my first draft.

In the "plotting versus pantsing" debate, I'm firmly in the plotting corner.

I don't disagree that some wonderful books are written by pantsers, but I'm not capable of doing that.

The following list is adapted from a list Larry Brookes put together at StoryFix.com some years ago. It sets up a solid framework for your story.

I'd recommend not starting your first draft until these questions are (substantially) answered:

How does your story open? What's the hook? What's keeping your readers eyes on the page

And then…

- what is the hero doing in their life before the first plot point? What is their "normal"?
- what stakes are established before the first plot point? Do both the Hero and Villain have stakes?
- what is your character's backstory? (I like to write a few pages of back story for new characters, to inform how they behave later in the story.) What's the villain's back story?
- does the villain have any positive qualities?
- what is foreshadowed prior to the first plot point?

What is the First Plot Point, pushing your hero through that metaphorical door and into your story?

- is it located properly within the story sequence?
- what makes it a one-way trip?
- how does it change the hero's agenda?
- what is the nature of the hero's new need?
- what is at stake relative to that need?
- what opposes the hero from meeting that

need?
- what does the villain have at stake?
- how will the reader side with the hero at this point?
- how does the hero respond to the villain?

What is the Mid-Point "what the—?" moment in your story?
- what new information is provided to the hero?
- how does this change the focus the story?
- does this pump up dramatic tension and pace?
- how does your hero begin to successfully attack this new variation on their quest?
- how does the villain respond to this attack?
- do the hero's inner demons come to bear on this attack?
- what is the all-is-lost lull just before the Second Plot Point?

What is the Second Plot Point in your story?
- how does this change or affect the hero's proactive role?
- how are the stakes of the story paid off?

- what are the key obstacles the hero needs to overcome to succeed?
- what will be the reader's emotional experience as the story concludes?

Spend some time working out the crime. (I write crime fiction.) Is there a missing person? A crime that needs solving? Has a friend gotten into a jam and neither of you want the police to get involved? It doesn't have to be complex. It can use unreliable witnesses (but drop something early in the story to point to their unreliability later).

And since you now know what pushed your hero on their journey, you can create an inciting incident early in the story to set up the passage through the metaphorical door.

The advantage of plotting out your story is that you *know* what clues are real and which are red herrings from the jump. Hold the big clues for important moments. Have your hero head down a false path and reveal a major clue at the midpoint to right their course.

Of course, by "reveal" I don't mean have it show up in the mail, handed to them on a silver platter. They have to work for it. It has to come at a cost, and it has to be a "this changes my path" moment.

The final clue needs to come at the end of Act Two, after the despair of "failing". This is the final piece of the puzzle the hero needs to resolve the case:

The "W" written in blood is actually an "M".

Or the grainy newspaper photo from 20 years ago shows a relationship unknown prior to that point.

Maybe a diary that was recovered early in Act Two is finally interpreted, revealing passage that explains it all.

Have fun with it.

Having a problem delaying the introduction of a key piece of info? Introduce a sloppy lab tech or a busy lab. Drop a piece of paper behind a desk, to be found at a more opportune time.

It's your book. It's your world to play with.

Once you've broken the story – when you know who is doing what to whom – write a couple of sentences for each of the scenes listed in this book: The hook, the inciting incident, the first and second plot points, the midpoint twist, both pinch points and the all is lost moment.

Then write a couple of sentences for the scenes leading up to those key scenes. And write a couple of sentences for the scenes *reacting* to those key scenes.

You've got the action part of your book plotted.

A final note.

After you've written a few books using this framework, you'll find that you can forget it. You'll instinctively know that your story needs a pinch point, or a midpoint twist as you plot it. You'll get better at teasing out the clues, both real and fake.

The structure isn't your story. Your story is the story. It'll be new, imaginative and quirky *without* the structure.

The structure makes it a smoother experience for your readers, removing any literary friction that might slow them down.

Good luck, and happy writing.

Structure

About the Author

Tony McFadden is a displaced Canadian now calling Australia home. He and his wife and two children live near the beaches, where he spends as much time as possible writing.

More about Tony and his writing can be found at
TonyMcFadden.net/mybooks, Facebook and Twitter.

Also by Tony McFadden:

G'Day LA • G'Day USA

Matt's War • Daly Battles: The Fall of Pyongyang • Target: Australia

Book 'Em - An Eamonn Shute Mystery • Unprotected Sax • Family Matters

Have Wormhole, Will Travel • Killing Time

Mac D Investigations
Mac D: Private Investigator • A Step Too Far • Hunter/Prey

McGinnis Investigations
The Murder of Jeremy Brookes • Number Fifteen

Nick Harding Cases
Batteries Not Included • Broken • Dead Tomorrow

www.ingramcontent.com/pod-product-compliance
Lightning Source LLC
Chambersburg PA
CBHW050321010526
44107CB00055B/2335